Regain Freedom
Daily Prayer Devotional

GW00726704

A
Practical Daily Devotional
That Will Inspire And Encourage
You To Live A Purposeful
And
Joyful Life.

Jacqueline Bent

ISBN 978-1-5272-7205-7

Published by: Jacqueline Bent

Editorial Production: The Editor's Chair

Printed in the United Kingdom

ENDORSEMENTS

It is with great pleasure and excitement that I take this opportunity to endorse this book. The author, Jacqueline Bent, is a woman known to me for many years. She is dedicated and selflessly committed to the body of Christ. She is contagious in her endeavour to walk the life of faith, to live and to love as Jesus taught us. She has earned the right of expression as she has already walked the walk of faith.

This book has foresight, insight and it will excite the reader to discover the promises of God and the surety of God's involvement in their lives for them to accomplish their purpose.

In a world where so much dirt is thrown at us which has tarnished our lives and blighted our view of God and his response to our cries, we celebrate the writing of Jacqueline Bent. Through her own experience of the journey of faith and trust in God, she has been inspired to write such beautiful words of comfort to help others on their journey to purpose.

I highly recommend this book to both men and women. It is not designed to be read and put down; but the purpose is to inspire the reader to a deeper walk with God and a greater commitment to press towards the mark of the highest calling in Christ Jesus. This is a balanced meal which should enable you to grow spiritual muscles. My prayer is that the Body of Christ will be a better place because of this book.

Overseer Joycelyn Vassel
Shammah International Ministries, UK

What particularly grabbed my attention was the word 'Freedom' in the title. I was curious to see whether this book would have the answers to assist me with decisions that I had to make regarding certain aspects of my life.

Once I started reading this book, I couldn't put it down and I believe you will feel the same. Every day I read the devotionals and prayed the prayers with anticipation of what the Lord would say to me that day.

The direction, life lessons, assurances and comfort that I experienced whilst reading this book will be with me for the rest of my life and my prayer is that you experience the same or better as a result of feasting on every word.

I intend to use this book as a 6-monthly reference and guidance tool to assist in keeping a check on my life decisions to ensure that I'm heading in the right direction and if need be, I will be making the necessary adjustments to stay on track.

My final word to you is to buy this book as I can assure you this will be the best investment that you have made in your entire life.

Joshua Barrett
SDGHSIP, UK

This is a MUST READ.
This book is a direct download from our Heavenly Father for such a time as this and is for anyone that needs a direct word from our Father. Whatever the situation or circumstance, that you may deem too difficult for you to continue in this life, l urge you to pick up this book and read it intently because once you read it daily and pray the prayers you will be restored in your spirit and receive a new lease of life.

Dr Karen McPherson
Action Chapel, Virginia USA

One word describes how Jacqueline draws on her own experiences of hope and faith and that's 'insightful'. She is an overcomer of obstacles and challenges and along the way she has Regained Freedom in Jesus Christ. This daily prayer devotional is an easy read of encouraging words and Bible scriptures. The devotional will enrich and bless you and draw you closer to God's purpose and will for your life, thus enabling the reader to 'Regain Freedom' in Christ.

Elder Beverley Chambers
Wembley Family Church, UK

It is my great delight to recommend this book as essential, necessary, and imperative for anyone who wants to fulfil their God given purpose for their life.

I have known Jacqueline Bent for many years and reading her daily prayer devotionals, I can tell that she is sharing her heart and passion of her love for people to grow and walk in progress, productivity and purpose.

This book will enlighten you on how to walk daily with the Lord, by the leading and guidance of the Holy Spirit. Jacqueline has made her writing very simplistic, but you will find it very effective in giving you daily instructions and encouragement that will empower you to tap into your God given gifts and talents and ultimately your life purpose. I found reading this daily prayer devotional so inspiring, easy to understand, reflective and challenging to my thinking.

Reverend Errol H. Brown
God's Humble Servant, UK

CONTENTS

DEDICATION

This work is dedicated to the only One who could have possibly enabled me to have the foresight to put pen to paper. The only One who had the confidence to believe that I could complete this work. He alone gave me the words letter by letter, word by word. An unprecedented thank you goes out to my Confidant and Best Friend, my Lord and Saviour, the Lord Jesus Christ.

Special HEARTFELT THANKS...

A very special heartfelt thanks to my precious son, Lorimar Joshua Charles. He has unconditionally loved me in the good and bad times. He has stood by me in my mess and through all my processing. The Lord has used him to be my eyes when I could not see straight. Even though he still doesn't understand some of the decisions that I've made, he has never judged me or loved me any less. He just continues to display the love of Christ. I give God thanks every day for the privilege of bringing into the world and nurturing such a fine young man.

HOW TO USE THIS
DAILY PRAYER DEVOTIONAL

You may choose to dip in and dip out of the pages. I've kept the daily readings and prayers short and concise to enable you to easily recall what you've read, at any time during the day.

Alternatively, you may choose to use the prayer devotional as a daily road map to guide you on your journey to 'Regain Freedom' and find your purpose.

I have included spaces for you to record your thoughts and revelations at the end of each entry.

However you choose to use this devotional book, my prayer is that you will be prompted and encouraged to become a better, stronger and more fulfilled person in every area of your life.

Now, journey with me as we explore the goodness of the Lord within the pages of this daily devotional book.

LAST BUT NOT LEAST...

To the Editor's Chair, I thank you all for the hours of hard work you have put into this work to produce the finished product. All of you worked tirelessly with me to ensure I didn't falter, faint or give up. There were many times that you encouraged and inspired me to keep going. Words fail me – thank you and thank you again and again.

INTRODUCTION

Through the many years that I've been teaching on fulfilling one's own purpose, I have found that many participants initially hit a stumbling block. This is usually when they are trying to overcome the realisation that they were born for a real purpose. They often find it hard to accept that they are not just here to make up numbers, aimlessly go through life and then die.

My own personal testimony is that after many years of feeling displaced and that I did not fit into the roles I found myself in, I entered into a journey of self-discovery. After a life-transforming experience, I recognised who I was and what my God-given purpose in life truly was. At this point in my life it became plainly obvious that I had been in preparation throughout my whole life and stepping into my God-purpose was the fulfilment of the many experiences I had been through.

My hope is that this book will serve to lead you on your own journey of self-discovery to identify and fulfil your God-given purpose. As you meditate on the daily words of encouragement and pray the daily prayers from a place of sincerity, I believe you will begin to discover your purpose and, upon this discovery, you will in turn naturally begin to experience a more joyful, restful and peaceful life.

KNOW THAT YOU ARE FEARFULLY AND WONDERFULLY MADE.

Psalm 139:14
'I will praise You, for I am fearfully and wonderfully made; Marvelous are Your works, and that my soul knows very well.'

I often wonder if we as believers understand the power of knowing that we are fearfully and wonderfully made. Did you know that you were uniquely designed by the Lord Himself? Your cells, tissues, organs, bones, and muscles were created by God. Let's not talk of your DNA and even your personality, your likes, and dislikes—these were all decided by the Lord before you entered this world. Know that there is no carbon copy of you anywhere in the universe. This makes you extraordinarily special!

In light of this, today I urge you to appreciate who you are. Do not compare yourself with anyone else ever again. Do not be intimidated by anyone else ever again. Know this one thing that the Lord has said about you; that you are 'fearfully and wonderfully made'.[1] I encourage you, from today, to start walking in the fullness of this amazing truth of God.

Prayer

Heavenly Father, I thank You for the truth that You've spoken about me. You said that I'm fearfully and wonderfully made. I believe it and I receive it. Father God, I will now walk in the knowledge that I am unique, special, and the handiwork of the greatest Creator of all time. In Jesus' name. Amen.

---

[1] *Job 22:28*
You will also declare a thing, and it will be established for you; so light will shine on your ways.

DAY 1 NOTES

_____

_____

_____

_____

_____

_____

_____

_____

_____

_____

_____

_____

_____

_____

_____

_____

_____

_____

_____

_____

_____

_____

_____

_____

YOU ARE MORE THAN A CONQUEROR.

Romans 8:37
'Yet in all these things we are more than conquerors through Him who loved us.'

Wow, what an amazing promise this is. You are more than you think you are. A conqueror is defined by Dictionary.com as someone who:

1. Acquires by force of arms, who wins in a war or overcomes a foreign land.
2. Overcomes by force, subdues or vanquishes to conquer an enemy.
3. Gains or wins by effort or personal appeal, and who gains the hearts of the audience.
4. Gains a victory over; surmounts; masters; overcomes; conquers their fear.

Do you see why I'm so excited that you are all the above and more? Because you have the Lord on your side, you are stronger than you think; you are an overcomer, a victor, and a winner in every area of your life.

Take courage from what I am saying to you. You really can walk away from that unhealthy relationship, you can start that business, you can start to learn a new skill, you can begin to homeschool your child. Why? Because the Lord has said that you are more than a conqueror and, because He loves you. He's your biggest cheerleader and nothing is going to change that.

Prayer

Father, You are my Lord and my Saviour. I believe that You are the One Who has given me the power and strength to fulfil all my heart's desires. You are my only source and I commit all my desires and aspirations into Your hands for You to answer in Your own infinite way. In Jesus' name. Amen.

DAY 2 NOTES

_____

_____

_____

_____

_____

_____

_____

_____

_____

_____

_____

_____

_____

_____

_____

_____

_____

_____

_____

_____

_____

_____

_____

_____

THE LORD IS ON YOUR SIDE.

1 Chronicles 22:18
'Is not the Lord your God with you? And has He not given you rest on every side? For He has given the inhabitants of the land into my hand, and the land is subdued before the Lord and before His people.'

Can you feel the presence of God? I know that in this busy and hectic world that we live in, it's often quite easy to forget that the Lord is right beside us in whatever situation we find ourselves in. When a situation or circumstance seems too much for you to bear on your own, please remember that you are not alone. We know this because the Lord said that He is right by your side, helping you carry the load. In times like this, just ask Him for direction and He will answer your prayer and a 'hallelujah praise of thanksgiving' is also to be submitted unto Him, in these times.

Prayer

I humbly come before You, Father God, to cry unto You in my time of need. I'm asking for Your divine direction and wisdom to resolve this impossible situation that I find myself in. I know it's only You who can offer the guidance I need right now, and so I offer this prayer with a pure heart. Speak Lord, speak Lord. I want to thank You in advance, Lord, for the answer to my prayer. I commit to follow Your instructions as given to me. In Jesus' name. Amen and amen.

DAY 3 NOTES

_____

_____

_____

_____

_____

_____

_____

_____

_____

_____

_____

_____

_____

_____

_____

_____

_____

_____

_____

_____

_____

_____

_____

_____

_____

_____

_____

WHY WORRY? IT'S ALREADY DONE.

Matthew 6:25-26
'Therefore, I say to you, do not worry about your life, what you will eat or what you will drink; nor about your body, what you will put on. Is not life more than food and the body more than clothing? Look at the birds of the air, for they neither sow nor reap nor gather into barns; yet your heavenly Father feeds them. Are you not of more value than they?'

Did you know that worry is a sin? The scripture tells us, 'Do not worry about your life.' That means every single aspect of your life, without exception. I don't know about you but I am often guilty of this sin. Time and time again I forget that the Lord will take care of my every need. And guess what? He'll do the same for you too. Will you join with me and commit to putting your every need into the Lord's hands for Him to deal with in His infinite timing and His infinite way?

Prayer

Lord, I repent of the sin of worry and unbelief and surrender myself to Your ability to take care of my every need and every aspect of my life. Help me to be more confident in the fact that You're in complete control. Lord, when my mind sways and my thoughts are negative and wander away from You, please remind me of who You are and that my help comes from You and only You. In Jesus' name. Amen.

DAY 4 NOTES

_____

_____

_____

_____

_____

_____

_____

_____

_____

_____

_____

_____

_____

_____

_____

_____

_____

_____

_____

_____

_____

_____

_____

_____

_____

THE LORD HAS NOT GIVEN US THE SPIRIT OF FEAR.

2 Timothy 1:7
'For God has not given us a spirit of fear, but of power and love and a sound mind.'

'Fear, Fear, Fear, who art thou?' Fear can be all-consuming to the point that you feel paralysed in your actions. It can creep up on you in such a way that you do not realise it until your life has abruptly come to an end. Not in the literal sense, but you might find that your plans and aspirations are affected because you are so terrified of moving forward in your life. You can quite easily find yourself in this state of fear for various reasons. For example, it could be as a result of an action that you took part in or that someone else took against you. You might have walked away from an unpleasant experience that now constantly plays on your mind. Whatever the reason that you find yourself in a state of fear, know that it has not been given to you by the Lord. And if that is the case then you can reject it, and begin to live a victorious life in the name of Christ Jesus.

Prayer

I give You all the glory, Lord, because I know that this state of fear that I find myself in is not something that You have orchestrated. If You have not given it to me then I do not have to dwell on it or receive it. Therefore, spirit of fear, I decree and declare that you have no hold on me and you must flee now in the mighty name of Jesus. Thank you, Lord, for the victory in Jesus' name. Amen.

DAY 5 NOTES

_____

_____

_____

_____

_____

_____

_____

_____

_____

_____

_____

_____

_____

_____

_____

_____

_____

_____

_____

_____

_____

_____

_____

_____

WEEPING MAY ENDURE FOR A NIGHT.

Psalm 30:5
'For His anger is but for a moment, His favor is for life; Weeping may endure for a night, but joy comes in the morning.'

The word 'weeping' may not always be meant in the physical sense. I believe that we can also weep in our spirit. Internally, we can feel suppressed and unable to control how we react when faced with the unexpected. It has been proven that when you are overreacting and when you are in a state of stress, it can lead to a host of medical issues. These include panic attacks, high blood pressure, and headaches to name a few. For you to overcome this weeping in your spirit, you need to remember who you are serving and consider whose report you believe in such times.[1] So, I urge you to remember that the above scripture clearly says that joy comes in the morning. Just believe it and receive it.

Prayer

Heavenly Father, when my heart is overwhelmed and my spirit-man is in turmoil, please help me to remember that You are the all-powerful, all-knowing and all-compassionate God Who will heal and see me through this place of pain that I'm in right now. I ask for the peace of God to be my portion now. Even though my thoughts and feelings are saying one thing, I ask that You enable me to concentrate on what Your Word says to me about my current circumstances. Help me to walk in the knowledge that I will come out of this dark place and come into Your marvellous light. In Jesus' name. Amen.

[1] *Mark 11:23*
For assuredly, I say to you, whoever says to this mountain, 'Be removed and be cast into the sea,' and does not doubt in his heart, but believes that those things he says will be done, he will have whatever he says.

DAY 6 NOTES

I WILL NEVER LEAVE YOU NOR FORSAKE YOU.

Hebrews 13:5
'Let your conduct be without covetousness; be content with such things as you have. For He Himself has said, "I will never leave you nor forsake you."'

The Word of God I'm quoting today is not only saying, 'I will never leave you nor forsake you' but also that it is well with your soul. The context is important. Before saying this, the scripture gives an instruction to not be 'covetous'. This means that we must be content with our lot in life. Therefore, we must not let whatever those around us have lead us to be envious of their possessions and lifestyle. We need to be content with who we are and what we own, such as with our gifts, talents, family/friends, and our material possessions. He has your back, therefore it's a comfort to know we can rest in this assurance.

If you can learn this, it will place you in a position of maturity and humility. In the fullness of time, as you walk in destiny and purpose, you will know without a shadow of a doubt that the Lord does not make mistakes because He has clearly said, 'I will never leave you nor forsake you.' Therefore, He will be right by your side guiding you and instructing you as you walk into the fullness of whatever He has prepared for you, and you alone.

Prayer

Lord of heaven and earth, please receive this prayer from me, your humble servant. I ask, Lord, that You remove whatever insecurities and doubts are overshadowing my ability to move forward into my divine destiny. Help me to stop coveting other people's gifts, talents, family/friends, and worldly possessions and comparing them with what I have been blessed with. In the name of Jesus, I receive complete healing and deliverance from these insecurities and the spirit of covetousness. I am now able to step into my destiny and purpose in the confidence that you 'will never leave me nor forsake me'. In Jesus' name. Amen.

DAY 7 NOTES

IF THE LORD CAN USE A DONKEY, WHY CAN'T HE USE YOU?

Numbers 22:23
'Now the donkey saw the Angel of the LORD standing in the way with His drawn sword in His hand, and the donkey turned aside out of the way and went into the field. So, Balaam struck the donkey to turn her back onto the road.'

Yes, it's true! If the Lord can use a donkey, why can't He use you? I used to often reflect on this and, probably like you, would reach the conclusion that I had no value and nothing of any great significance to contribute to any worthwhile activity. However, one day I woke up and realised that even the smallest of acts, such as giving someone a hug or a smile or simply saying 'Hello' to a stranger can often be a lifesaver.

These gestures may seem small on the surface but can have a great impact on the recipient, especially if they are experiencing a period of loneliness, confusion, or emotional pain. I could have given grander examples — but who defines what grand gestures are, anyway? The reason I offered these examples, is to help you understand that even in the smallest of acts, the Lord can use you to save lives and make a difference.

So, please stop thinking that you are not important enough, intelligent enough, pretty enough, and all the other enoughs. Remember that if the Lord can use a donkey, He can use you!

Prayer

Heavenly Father, I ask that You hear my prayer as I ask You to use me in whatever capacity You see fit. I come before You as a yielded and broken vessel, ready to be obedient to Your instructions. Please give me the wisdom and ability to move forward in complete confidence and in the knowledge that as a yielded and broken vessel, I am good enough to be used by You just as I am, faults and all. In Jesus' name. Amen.

DAY 8 NOTES

YOU'RE IN YOUR SEASON OF PROCESSING.

1 Samuel 1:20
'So, it came to pass in the process of time that Hannah conceived and bore a son, and called his name Samuel, saying, "Because I have asked for him from the Lord."'

Hannah was in her season of processing when she cried out to the Lord to have a child. By the end of her processing, her relationship with the Lord was unshakable and steadfast. During this period, she drew extremely close to the Lord, to the point where she would have done whatever it took to experience the joy of motherhood and to be released from the reproach of not bearing a child for her husband.

We know that there was someone who constantly reminded her of her barren position — Peninnah. She was Hannah's husband's other wife and had already borne him many children.[1] How many of you may have a Peninnah in your life? What should you do in such a situation? Well, you should simply do what Hannah did — take your issue to the Lord in prayer. Pray, pray and pray until you see results. Pray until you see the manifestation of your prayer right in front of your eyes. Hannah eventually saw the answer to her prayers. Hannah eventually bore a son. She named him Samuel, who she then dedicated back to the Lord, for Him to use Samuel for His reasonable service.

---

[1] 1 Samuel 1: 6-7
And her rival also provoked her severely, to make her miserable, because the LORD had closed her womb. So it was, year by year, when she went up to the house of the LORD, that she provoked her; therefore, she wept and did not eat.

So, the key here is to pray without ceasing.[2] Once your prayer has been answered, give the Lord thanks by dedicating and committing the manifestation of your answered prayer back to Him. By doing this, you will have opened the door to abundant blessings in all areas of your life.

Prayer

Father God, You know the end from the beginning. You knew that I would be coming to Your throne of grace with the issue that's on my heart. I ask, Father God, that You search my heart and uproot any unhealthy condition that You know is hindering me from experiencing the answer to my heartfelt prayer. When You show me what the hindrance is, Lord, give me the will and desire to let it go in Jesus' name. I thank You, Lord, in advance for the manifestation of my prayer, and as a way of showing you my complete sincerity, I promise that I will dedicate the answer to my prayer back to You with thanksgiving. In Jesus' name. Amen.

---

[2] *1 Thessalonians 5:17*
Pray without ceasing.

DAY 9 NOTES

FORGIVE AND LET GO, THAT'S THE GREATEST DELIVERANCE OF ALL.

Matthew 6:15
'But if you do not forgive men their trespasses, neither will your Father forgive your trespasses.'

At times, it seems as if being able to walk in a constant state of forgiveness is impossible. This is usually because we tend to repeatedly replay the situation that has led to the feeling of unforgiveness in our minds.

However, you'll eventually realise that the person who hurt you is quite happily getting on with their life. You're the only one who is still stuck in the cycle of unforgiveness and pain. This is the time to be praying constantly for healing and deliverance so that your spirit will begin to soften towards that person and eventually you'll be able to release them and the pain that they have caused you.

Most importantly, once you've reached this state of forgiveness, the scripture says, 'Your Father will forgive your trespasses.' Hallelujah! This alone will make the pain of going through the whole cycle of forgiveness worthwhile as you learn this valuable lesson.

Prayer

Father God, I cry out to You to reach into the depths of my soul to uproot the spirit of unforgiveness that I feel towards .... (name the person/s involved). Wash me in Your Son's precious blood so that I may be cleansed from all unrighteous thoughts and feelings towards .... (name the person/s involved). I know that these feelings are not of God and, Father, as I want to ultimately receive the gift of Your forgiveness, I surrender my will and all my unhealthy feelings of unforgiveness to You so that You can start the healing and deliverance process in me. Father, I ask that if I fail at any time during this process, You'll have mercy on me, pick me up, and set me back on the path of healing and deliverance. In Jesus' name. Amen.

DAY 10 NOTES

THE WEALTH OF THE WICKED IS WAITING FOR YOU.

Deuteronomy 8:18
'And you shall remember the Lord your God, for it is He who gives you the power to get wealth ...'

Most people see wealth in monetary terms and not in a wider sense, for instance, as health, strength, being able to support the needs of your family, or peace of mind. These are all types of wealth, and so too are answers to specific prayers, a happy marriage or recovering successfully from a life-threatening illness. Why do we almost always exclusively consider only money as wealth when we have so many other invaluable blessings to be grateful for? Well, I'm glad you asked. Putting it mildly, we have been conditioned by society and the circumstances that we find ourselves in, to rely on our intellect and abilities to provide for our own financial needs by ourselves, rather than to rely on the Lord to supply all of our needs.

However, if you make a conscious decision to be in a constant state of gratitude for the types of 'wealth' named above, and a whole lot of other situations that are just as valid, this will serve to please the Lord tremendously and lead Him to want to provide for all your needs, including your finances.

Further, walking in a state of gratitude has endless benefits. To name a few of these: improved psychological and physical health, better sleep, others who walk in a state of gratitude will gravitate towards you, your self-esteem will improve, and you'll experience improved relationships. The list goes on and on but I think you get the idea.

So, the key here is to be forever grateful for what you have and to remember that your wealthy place is how you define it. As a result of this way of thinking, the Lord will supply all your needs and more.[1]

Prayer

Father, please accept this sincere prayer as I ask for You to search my heart. Bring to my remembrance any situation that I've been involved in where I have not completely trusted You in relation to being in my wealthy place, wherever and whatever that might be. You know everything and You see everything, so I want to apologise from the bottom of my heart. I present to you a heart of thanksgiving and gratitude for what You're about to do in my life. In Jesus' name. Amen.

---

[1] *Philippians 4:19*
And my God shall supply all your needs according to His riches in glory by Christ Jesus.

DAY 11 NOTES

REFLECT, REFLECT, REFLECT.

Nehemiah 1:5
'And I said: "I pray, Lord God of heaven, O great and awesome God,
you who keep Your covenant and mercy with those who love You and
observe Your commandments.'

It's often good to reflect on where you've been and where you intend
to go in the future. Reflection can sometimes cause you to experience
some form of pain and regret, especially when you consider how your
life has turned out due to past decisions, mistakes, and relationships.

But take heart. Going through a period of reflection should be seen
as a positive thing to do because it can often focus your mind on the
direction you should be going in. At this stage of the process, prayer
is of paramount importance. Ensuring that you're hearing clearly
from God during this season is a requirement because without the
Lord's direction you could very well end up making the same errors
and mistakes again. Getting caught up in this vicious cycle is exactly
how the enemy can ensnare you into repeating mistakes. This
behaviour is precisely the sort that will leave you broken, confused,
and even fearful of what the future holds for you.

However, I'm here to let you know that we serve a God of second
chances who knows the end from the beginning.[1] So, please be
assured that He will hear your prayers and He will answer them
when and how He sees fit.

---

[1] *John 1:9*
If we confess our sins, He is faithful and just to forgive us our sins and to cleanse us from
all unrighteousness.

Prayer

As the scriptures say, You are a God Who cannot lie and You have promised me that I shall be the head and not the tail, above and not beneath. So, Father God, I cut off the spirit of being the tail and the spirit of being beneath. I claim all the blessings that are mine to claim. I ask for divine inspiration and divine wisdom. Open up my spiritual ears, Lord, and I ask that You speak to me loudly and clearly in whatever way You deem necessary, be it through the Bible, by speaking to someone, through a song, through a television programme or through a billboard. These are but a few examples, Lord, but in essence, I'm asking you to speak to me in Jesus' name. Amen.

DAY 12 NOTES

LIVING A LIFE OF PURPOSE IS WHAT YOU'RE MEANT TO BE DOING.

Exodus 9:16
'But indeed, for this purpose, I have raised you up, that I may show My power in you, and that My name may be declared in all the earth.'

Fulfilling your life purpose is not always easy, especially when you don't know what your life purpose is. Are you asking yourself any of the following questions: 'What is the reason for my very existence? Why has the Lord sent me to the earth? I've been set apart but what does the Lord want me to accomplish on His behalf?' If you are asking yourself any of these questions and can't seem to find any answers, let me let you in on a little secret. There is only one sure way to find the answers to your questions. Are you ready for this? I want you to ask yourself this very simple question and the first thought that comes into your mind is the answer you're looking for. Here we go, 'What's that burning activity in your spirit that you would carry out even if you didn't get paid?' When the majority of people answer this question, the answer is invariably (but not always) the activity that they quite happily do in their leisure time, such as their hobby. There you go! Did you see how simple that was?

Does the answer seem quite overwhelming and completely out of your depth? That's good because if you can accomplish your life purpose in your strength then the Lord will not get the glory and He will probably not be in this with you.

Now that you have the answer to your questions, you have to decide on the way forward. It may well be quite a daunting prospect for you and the first thing you must do is pray and ask the Lord for His guidance. Ask Him for the road map; this will be the plan that you have to follow to execute and fulfil your life purpose. Be sure to listen very carefully to what He is saying to you and be prepared to hear some things that you do not want to hear. In all of this, wait for the right time as this is paramount to the success of fulfilling your life purpose: remember, our timing is not the Lord's timing.[1] Be warned – do not run ahead without the Lord's guidance as you are guaranteed to fail or at a minimum achieve some mediocre success. You will not attain the fullness of what you have set out to achieve.

Having said all this, the Lord will not force you into fulfilling your life purpose. He gives us free will in all things, so if you choose not to go along with His plan for your life, He will simply raise someone else up in your place. I don't say this to make you uneasy but to explain to you the reality of the situation.

Now, let's offer up a prayer to the Lord for His guidance, strength, and wisdom to fulfil your life purpose.

Prayer

Lord God, I thank You for answering my prayer. Now that You have revealed my life's purpose to me, I ask You, Lord, for the blueprint that You have for me to fulfil and accomplish it. I thank You in advance for sending the right people, the resources, and for giving me the determination, courage, and confidence to go through the process to the very end. I ask for the wisdom to know when You are speaking, when to proceed and when to pause. Father, You are worthy to be praised in all things and I thank You for wanting to use me in such a profound way to advance the things of God on earth. I commit to being faithful in all that You ask me to do. I promise to fulfil all that You would have me do in the right spirit and the knowledge that, at all times, You are in control and not I. In Jesus' name. Amen.

---

[1] *Ecclesiastes 3:1*
  To everything there is a season, A time for every purpose under heaven.

DAY 13 NOTES

_____

_____

_____

_____

_____

_____

_____

_____

_____

_____

_____

_____

_____

_____

_____

_____

_____

_____

_____

_____

_____

_____

_____

_____

_____

ARE YOU WAITING ON THE LORD FOR AN ANSWER TO PRAYER?

Ecclesiastes 3:1
'To everything, there is a season...'

Have you been praying for a relatively long time about a certain situation and the answer to that prayer has not yet come? Are you becoming increasingly frustrated because you feel that the Lord is ignoring your prayer? Have you been praying from a place of sincerity but are now beginning to feel desperation creeping in?

Well, I have news for you: the Lord has heard your prayer. It simply may be that if He answered your prayer right now it could be to your detriment. Perhaps what you're praying for is not God's best and He wants to bless you in another way far beyond what you can even imagine.

Be encouraged. Keep trusting and keep waiting on the Lord and He will answer that prayer according to His timing. Remember that the Lord's timing is not our timing so rest assured He will reveal the answer to your prayer at the best time for you. I urge you to be both confident that He will not let you down and expectant in your time of waiting. Have the confidence to know that the revelation of the answer to your prayer is forthcoming.

Prayer

Father God, You are worthy to be praised and there is none like You in all the earth. I ask that You forgive me for not trusting and believing in You enough to know that You are my Saviour and that Your ways and Your timing are far above what I can even begin to understand. I will wait patiently for Your answer to my prayer, Lord. In my waiting, I will praise You and offer up thanksgiving in advance of what You're about to do for me. In Jesus' name. Amen.

DAY 14 NOTES

YOUR CHILDREN ARE A REFLECTION OF YOU.

Luke 2:49
'And He said to them, "Why did you seek Me? Did you not know that I must be about My Father's business?"'

The Bible says, 'Train up a child in the way that he should go, and when he is old he will not depart from it.'[1] The above scripture talks about a young Jesus who was found by His anxious parents in a temple in Jerusalem. He was sitting among the teachers, both listening to them and asking them questions. The scriptures go on to say that all who heard Him were astonished at His understanding and answers. This is a clear demonstration of a child going about His Father's business and showing the traits of a younger version of His Father. The young Jesus was emulating the lessons and wisdom that His Father had taught Him before He came to the earth. He was undoubtedly a mini version of His Father.

What we can take away from the above example is that whichever principles and lessons a child is shown and taught through their development stages will invariably be what they exhibit in their adult life. Therefore, if you are a parent please be mindful of the following:

1. The way you speak to your children

2. The principles and values that you not only teach your children but demonstrate

3. The way you treat others and speak to them in front of your children

---

[1] *Proverbs 22:6*
Train up a child in the way he should go, and when he is old, he will not depart from it.

Of, course, this list is not exhaustive but it illustrates my point. You are your children's most important teacher and therefore you have the huge responsibility of moulding, making, and shaping your children into the people that they will eventually become in adulthood.

The greatest gift of all you can both demonstrate and give to your children is unconditional love for all mankind, no matter their race, gender, religion, sexual orientation, marital status or disability.

Prayer

I come before You, Father God, and I repent of anything that I may have said or demonstrated to my children that does not glorify You. I ask for the wisdom, knowledge and the keys to be the Godly parent that I desire to be and that You have ordained for me to be. Send me help in this area, Lord God. Send Godly women and men who will be happy to share their wisdom, knowledge and experience with me and to mentor me in the area of parenting. Father, I thank You in advance for hearing my prayer and for answering as You see fit. In Jesus' name. Amen.

DAY 15 NOTES

EGYPT IS NOW BEHIND YOU.

Joshua 4:23
'For the Lord, your God dried up the waters of the Jordan before you until you had crossed over, as the Lord your God did to the Red Sea, which He dried up before us until we had crossed over.'

The Lord loves you so much that He'll turn an impossible situation into something possible. How could it be that the Lord parted not only one but two 'seas' to rescue His children in their time of need? Plainly and simply, He did it out of love and compassion. Just think – if He could do the impossible for the children of Israel after all their failings and disobedience, why wouldn't He do the same for you?

The impossible situation that I'm referring to is the gift of salvation. This is the greatest gift that you will ever receive as long as you are living on earth. In His infinite kindness, the Lord has saved you from darkness and brought you into His marvellous light. Why would you even consider going back to Egypt? A barren place, a place of unfruitfulness, a place where you are not valued, a place of hardship, and a place of suffering?

If you are considering drawing back, I urge you to reconsider and not forget all the benefits that are rightfully yours as a child of the King of Kings and the Lord of Lords. You walk in the authority of an ambassador. As an ambassador, you have the right to diplomatic immunity on the earth. These are your Kingdom rights. At any time you can call on the great 'I Am' and He will be to you whatever you need Him to be at that moment in time. He will be your doctor, your lawyer, your provider, your peace, and anything or anyone else you need Him to be.

I urge you to not give up on Him for He has not given up on you. Whatever you are going through right now, please do not be discouraged. Remember that the earth is your temporary home and as a citizen of a holy nation and a sojourner, you are merely passing through on the way to your heavenly home. The journey may be tough at times but you have a God Who will never fail you and will never leave you. Just trust and obey Him and He will do the rest.

Prayer

Lord, prepare me to be holy and acceptable to You. In all my failings and disobedience, You still saw it fit to give me that sweet gift of salvation. I humbly ask, Lord, that You keep me strong in my spirit and looking to You at all times. You are the author and finisher of my faith. I recognise that I cannot do anything out of my own strength. I need Your guidance and assistance through the Comforter, the Holy Spirit, now and forevermore. In Jesus' name. Amen.

DAY 16 NOTES

DO NOT BE A BUTLER.

Genesis 40:23
'Yet the chief butler did not remember Joseph, but forgot him.'

Have you ever done someone a huge favour or gone out of your way to accommodate someone in their time of need only to be sidelined when you call on that person to return the favour or kind act? Or have you been that person who has not been available for someone in their time of need after they had gone out of their way to assist you when you needed help? Sometimes as human beings we behave in a way that demonstrates that we are extremely selfish and mean-spirited. The feeling of being sidelined or rejected can be painful for the recipient so why would you want to inflict pain on top of the pain that they are already experiencing?

Please, do not behave in the same way as the chief butler who did not remember Joseph as he had promised while they were in prison together. Yes, the butler did eventually remember Joseph – as an afterthought when he was prompted by his master's plight of needing a dream interpreted.

Are you willing to commit to displaying compassion and love to all those around you who need help and assistance? Especially remembering those who stood by your side when you had a burden or a crisis in your life. Remember that they chose to stay by your side and help you through. They did not turn their backs on you.

Prayer

Father God, I repent of any selfish behaviour that I've shown toward anyone who has needed me to help them. Forgive me for whenever I have decided to turn away and not get involved when they reached out for my help. Father, give me the mind of Christ, so I can display Your loving kindness to all those around me whether it is convenient or not.

I commit to being that friend or confidant that others can rely on. Help me, Lord, to be that person who will always have a listening ear and be willing to give the time that is needed to help and assist wherever and whenever I can. In Jesus' name. Amen.

DAY 17 NOTES

THE LORD WILL OPEN YOUR EYES.

Genesis 30:31-32
'So he said, "What shall I give you?"
And Jacob said, "You shall not give me anything. If you will do this
thing for me, I will again feed and keep your flocks: Let me pass through
all your flock today, removing from there all the speckled and spotted
sheep, and all the brown ones among the lambs, and the spotted and
speckled among the goats; and these shall be my wages."'

Jacob was given an ingenious idea by the Lord that in the natural
made absolutely no sense at all. His father-in-law probably thought
that he had once more hoodwinked Jacob with another deceitful act
that he would gain from. However, Jacob had other plans. He had
an unction that by following this unusual plan, he would come out of
it a very wealthy man indeed, and he most certainly did.

The lesson here is that the Lord at times will prompt you to do
something that makes no sense at all. It might even border on the
edge of lunacy and people around you may believe that you are
crazy. However, the Lord is not an author of confusion or disorder.
If the Lord has prompted it, that crazy act that no one understands
may be all you need. In your act of obedience, the outcome of your
actions that are perceived by many as crazy and foolish will be where
your spiritual, financial, or health breakthrough is discovered. So,
take heart and believe that the Lord is the One Who gave you that
instruction and/or idea. Just trust and believe. Do not fear or let
double-mindedness get in the way of your breakthrough.

Jacob certainly came away with an abundance of blessings from the
unusual request he made to his father-in-law. You can have the same
testimony if you ever find yourself in a similar position. Just trust
and believe in the Lord at times like this.

Take the time to pray through what you've been told to do so that you can have peace within your spirit. Once you are confident that it is the Lord speaking to you, then go for it and never look back.

Prayer

Heavenly Father, You are a God of uniqueness and creativity. The instruction/idea that you have given me does not make sense in the slightest but I come against this fear that is trying to take over my mind and that is trying to grip me into the depths of doubt and despair. I reject it in the name of Jesus. I replace fear and doubt with confidence and the resilience that is needed to pursue and perform the instruction that You've given me. Oh Lord, I do not want to be put to shame and therefore I claim the victory in the mighty name of Jesus. Amen and amen.

DAY 18 NOTES

GET THEE BEHIND ME, SATAN.

Luke 4:13
'Now when the devil had ended every temptation, he departed from Him until an opportune time.'

When the devil tries to tempt you to do or say something that you know is against your Christian values or morals, remember that Jesus was also tempted by the devil and He passed the test. Is there any reason why you cannot do the same and pass the test when you're tempted? Jesus was no different than you or I. The only difference was that He was clear and confident in who He was. That is, He was a man who was not lacking in faith, and He had a very strong relationship with His Father in heaven.

The devil is cunning and will stop at nothing to expose you and I to situations that, if we took part in and/or acted upon, would break our witness as believers, to those around us. Further, the damage that would occur to our faith in the Lord would have serious repercussions and lead to a backslidden condition. Consider it – is it really worth the possible outcome to succumb to any sort of temptation? I say, no, it isn't. However, if you've been tempted and succumbed to temptation, do not feel condemned because you serve a God of second chances.[1]

---

1. *1 John 1:9*
   If we confess our sins, He is faithful and just to forgive us our sins and to cleanse us from all unrighteousness.

The Lord is merciful and His mercies endure forever.[2] Even though we may not deserve it, He has said that He will never leave nor forsake us.[3] Hallelujah! What amazing promises these are. The Lord is saying that He is there to protect and guide you no matter what, as long as you repent of your sin(s), He is willing to wipe the slate clean and put whatever it is you are asking forgiveness for into the sea of forgetfulness. He can do this because He has never stopped loving you whatever condition you're in spiritually.

The key here is repentance. Once you repent with a sincere heart the Lord will do the rest. He doesn't need our help. He has already done everything that needs to be done on the cross; just accept it, and do not dwell on your current or past mistakes but concentrate on the road that is ahead of you. That road is filled with an abundance of blessings – even more than you can imagine or comprehend.

Prayer

I need you, Father, more than I can articulate in words. You know that my heart is to serve You in spirit and truth. I know that sometimes I fail miserably. I can only say to You, Lord, please hear my prayer and cry of repentance from my inner being. I ask for Your mercy and forgiveness at this time. Help me, Lord, to be able to walk away from any unhealthy situation that may lead me to be tempted to fall into sin. The devil thinks that he is strong but I know who has the ultimate say, Lord. You are a God Who cannot lie and if You said that I'm forgiven then I receive it and I believe it. In Jesus' name. Amen.

---

2. *Psalm 89:1*
   I will sing of the mercies of the Lord forever; With my mouth will I make known Your faithfulness to all generations.

3 *Hebrews 13:5*
   Let your conduct be without covetousness; be content with such things as you have. For He Himself has said, "I will never leave you nor forsake you."

DAY 19 NOTES

_____

_____

_____

_____

_____

_____

_____

_____

_____

_____

_____

_____

_____

_____

_____

_____

_____

_____

_____

_____

_____

_____

JEZEBEL IS IN TROUBLE.

2 Kings 9:10
'The dogs shall eat Jezebel on the plot of ground at Jezreel, and there shall be none to bury her. And he opened the door and fled.'

Is there someone in your life that is deliberately setting out to disrespect or harm you in any way possible? This person is on assignment to see you fail and be destroyed but I'm here to tell you that the Lord has your back. Just like Jezebel came to a sorry end, this person will also experience a sorry end. Now, let me clarify. I'm not saying that this person is going to physically die. However, they will probably experience unexpected challenges. For instance, losing a much-loved job, forever lacking in their finances or always hankering after positions of power but never quite achieving this goal. These are just examples. Do not try to challenge this person. Simply make your request known to the Lord and He will do the rest. The Bible says that revenge belongs to the Lord.[1] Leave revenge to Him. He knows what He's doing. Have no fear and lose no sleep because the Jezebel in your life will meet with the vengeance of God Almighty.

You might be saying, 'Yes, it's alright for you to be saying this, you don't understand the pain and ridicule that I'm going through.' My answer to you is, 'Yes, I do.' My character, my family, my business, my appearance, and a whole lot more have been subjected to criticism and ridicule. I used to take offence and seek in my heart to get the person back for what they were doing to me. The embarrassment was often incredibly

---

1 *Romans 12:19*
  Beloved, do not avenge yourselves, but rather give place to wrath; for it is written, "Vengeance is Mine, I will repay," says the Lord.

painful to the point that I could feel my whole body recoiling in this unbelievable feeling of sickness – it would consume my total being.

However, praise be to God, my deliverance came when the Lord told me in His Word not to let my heart be troubled because He would take care of everything concerning me. He did just that in miraculous ways that only He could have planned. So, I've been sent to tell you not to be discouraged because Jezebel's days are numbered. Just relax, trust, and believe the Word of God because He's in control and will not let you be put to shame or leave you in distress.

Prayer

Lord, when my enemies come against me, I simply ask You to be my avenger. I ask that You bring to my remembrance that You are in control of the situation and that You will deal with the root of the matter, Jezebel. I trust that You will do this in Your infinite timing. I will not let my heart be troubled because You have promised in Your Word that revenge is Yours. I'll leave the revenge to You, Father God. I now enter into a period of rest, confident that You're going to work everything out for my good. Lord, I thank You in advance for the testimony that I'll be able to share with the world of Your goodness and faithfulness. In Jesus' name. Amen and amen.

DAY 20 NOTES

THE ESTHER ANOINTING.

Esther 2:17
'The king loved Esther more than all the other women, and she obtained grace and favor in his sight more than all the virgins; so, he set the royal crown upon her head and made her queen instead of Vashti.'

How many of you have heard the saying that favour is not fair? This is true when it comes to the things of God. He lets the rain (blessings) fall on the just and the unjust.[1] He does not have favourites but He will use His powers to put some of His children into positions of influence in order for His will to be carried out. This was the case when Esther was shown more favour than the other virgins whilst she was in preparation to be presented to the king. The Lord placed Esther in such a position for His glory because He was going to use Esther to deliver His people from the king's evil clutches.

Have you ever found yourself in a position of favour and not been able to humanly understand or explain how you found yourself in such a position in the first place? It could well be that the Lord has a work for you to do right where you find yourself. If you ever find yourself in such a position, I would urge you to prayerfully enquire of the Lord as to the reason He has allowed you the privilege of being in that place or position. He will answer you and He'll then leave it up to you to decide whether or not you are prepared to fulfil the assignment that He has prepared for you to carry out. Esther found herself in the same position when her uncle Mordecai revealed to her the reason she had been shown favour by the king. Esther accepted her assignment. Will you?

---

[1] *Matthew 5:45*
that you may be sons of your Father in heaven; for He makes His sun rise on the evil and on the good, and sends rain on the just and on the unjust.

Prayer

Lord, I'm enquiring of You today as I find myself in a position of favour that only You could have orchestrated. Lord, I ask that You reveal to me the reason that I find myself in such a position. I promise that Your will, not my will, shall be done. I ask for the grace and the supernatural ability to fulfil the assignment that is before me as I know that without these qualities and You by my side, I am certain that I will fail. Lord, I'd like to thank You in advance for answering my prayer and for choosing me, Your humble servant, to carry out the assignment that is before me. In Jesus' name. Amen.

DAY 21 NOTES

WHOSE REPORT DO YOU BELIEVE?

Mark 9:24
'Immediately the father of the child cried out and said with tears, "Lord, I believe; help my unbelief!"'

The father in this scripture suffered from what many of us as believers can identify with. Yes, it's that old subject that we shy away from – unbelief. We say on one hand that we trust God in all things, we quote all the relevant scriptures, say the right things, yet sometimes our actions make all of that questionable. A situation may occur where our faith has to be demonstrated publicly or even within our hearts between us and the Lord, and we fail miserably. Why is this?

My take on all of this is that it's because we have not grounded ourselves enough in the Word of God and have not developed an unshakable, solid relationship with Him. Take a few minutes now to consider what I'm saying and I think you'll agree with me…

Well, am I wrong or right?

Take heart and be encouraged. The Lord already knows all our weaknesses and flaws. Hallelujah! Praise be to God. He has not condemned us and, therefore, in turn, we should not be condemning ourselves. It's quite simple – just come before the Lord with a heart of repentance. Ask Him for forgiveness and seek His guidance in how you can dig deeper into His Word. From this, your prayer life and relationship with Him will go from strength to strength. One practical idea is to look online for study tools such as a daily Bible study programme. Alternatively, search in your Bible as some of them have daily Bible study suggestions in the reference section.

Praise be to God! The Lord is merciful and true to His Word. Just trust and obey Him because there is no other way.

Prayer

Precious Father, I come before You with a heart of repentance and I humbly ask that You forgive me for not trusting and believing in the promises that You've given me in your Word, the Bible. How can I ever begin to express what's in my heart? Father, I know that You are a gracious, just, and forgiving God. My relationship with You is the most important thing in my whole life, so Father God please direct me to the right place where I will find the tools that I need to begin to study Your Word with ease, liberty, and an open heart. Thank You, Lord, that You have set me on this exciting road of discovery. I ask for the determination to stay on course. Thank You, Lord, that the result is that I will have a deeper faith in You and as a result of this our relationship will be unshakable. In Jesus' name. Amen.

DAY 22 NOTES

_____

_____

_____

_____

_____

_____

_____

_____

_____

_____

_____

_____

_____

_____

_____

_____

_____

_____

_____

_____

_____

_____

_____

LOOK TO THE HILLS WHERE YOUR HELP COMES FROM.

Genesis 15:3-4
'Then Abram said, "Look, You have given me no offspring; indeed one born in my house is my heir!" 4 And behold, the word of the LORD came to him, saying, "This one shall not be your heir, but one who will come from your own body shall be your heir.""

Here we go again, running ahead of God! We want the blessing right now and our impatience means that we often miss the biggest blessing of all because we have run ahead of God.

I'm going to be transparent once more. Quite some time ago, I was believing in God that a certain situation would resolve itself but it seemed to be taking forever to be made right, so I decided to take matters into my own hands. To this day I am still paying the price for being impatient and taking the place of God. I know I'm forgiven and I know that the Lord is going to make a way where there seems to be no way but it has been a painful experience to go through, all because I was not willing to wait for the Lord's best timing to work everything out.

Abram displayed the same impatience and ran ahead of God. He had a child with his servant instead of waiting to have the child that God had promised with his wife. Like me, Abram paid the price for being disobedient and impatient.

Day 23

Do you see how we are walking on very dangerous ground when we do not wait on the Lord's perfect timing? If this is you today, be encouraged – the Lord hears your cry and He will give you the desires of your heart.[1] I urge you to trust and obey Him and in the fullness of time, He will answer your prayer in a way that only He can. He'll answer in His own way so that He will get all the glory, praise, and adoration from the fruit of your lips.

Prayer

Heavenly Father, please hear my cry as I ask You to endow me with a spirit of obedience and patience. I acknowledge that You know best and that Your timing is perfect in all things. I know that I could not ask for a better, more loving Father Who wants the very best for me at all times. I sometimes forget this but hallelujah, praise be to God, You are still right by my side loving and forgiving me. I'd like to thank You in advance for the answer to my prayer and I pledge to wait on Your perfect timing in all that I desire from You. In Jesus' name. Amen and amen.

---

[1] *Psalm 37:4*
Delight yourself also in the Lord, And He shall give you the desires of your heart.

DAY 23 NOTES

THE LORD WILL DIRECT YOU.

Proverbs 3:6
'In all your ways acknowledge Him, And He shall direct your paths.'

As we go about our daily lives, let's try to remember the goodness of the Lord at all times. In the good times and in the bad times He is still the Lord on high. He is still our sustainer, He is still the lily of the valley and the great morning star. He is still the rock in everything concerning our lives. When you're at a crossroad in life, all seems to be lost, and you really don't know which way to turn, just send up a prayer and a hallelujah praise and the Lord will direct your path, often in the most extraordinary ways.

My mind takes me to the book of Judges when the prophetess Deborah led the children of Israel into battle. There was no way to predict the outcome of the battle but Deborah and Barak – a military commander in the army – went into battle singing a victory song in anticipation that the Lord had already gone before them and that the battle had already been won.

Praise be to God, they did not waver or doubt because the children of Israel had already seen the victory in the spiritual realm before it had been won in the natural. As children of God, this is the level of faith that we should be aspiring to, an unwavering faith that knows that the Lord is indeed directing our every step along the path of our lives. So, even in the smallest of things, let's make it a point of duty to acknowledge the Lord because He is worthy to be praised, and ultimately He knows best.

Prayer

You are worthy to be praised, Father God, and there is none like You in all the earth. Give me the faith to know that whatever situation or circumstance I find myself in, I need to walk in the knowledge that You are right there beside me guiding and directing the path of my life. I acknowledge that You know best and whatever the outcome of my walk in this life, Father God, I know that You have my very best interests at heart at all times. So, I thank You, Lord, for the gift of life. I dedicate my life to You, for You to use me as you see fit. In Jesus' name. Amen.

DAY 24 NOTES

_____

_____

_____

_____

_____

_____

_____

_____

_____

_____

_____

_____

_____

_____

_____

_____

_____

_____

_____

_____

_____

_____

_____

YOU'RE ON THE WINNING SIDE.

Job 1:9-12

'So Satan answered the LORD and said, "Does Job fear God for nothing? Have You not made a hedge around him, around his household, and around all that he has on every side? You have blessed the work of his hands, and his possessions have increased in the land. But now, stretch out Your hand and touch all that he has, and he will surely curse You to Your face!" And the LORD said to Satan, "Behold, all that he has is in your power; only do not lay a hand on his person." So, Satan went out from the presence of the LORD.'

Have you ever felt at times that all is against you, nothing seems to be going right for you, everything you put your hand to falls apart or fails at the last minute and you just can't figure out what the root of the problem is? It could well be that you are in a period of testing, just as Job found himself in. I'm here to tell you, please do not despair. You are on the winning side because the Lord has your back. He is simply allowing the situation to evolve to either teach you something or to test some traits that you have. In Job's case, it was his faithfulness and relationship with the Lord.

Why, you might ask yourself, would the Lord ever want to go to these lengths? Well, the answer is simply that you may never know until we go to glory because He is sovereign and He can and does do things in His own way. He certainly doesn't need our permission and His ways are clearly not our ways. He knows best, so whatever the outcome of our period of testing, we should rest assured in the knowledge that we are on the winning side, no matter what happens.

Prayer

Lord, You know everything and You see everything. Father, whatever situation I find myself in, I know You are right there with me because You have allowed me to be placed in that situation for a reason that I may never know. However, through it all, I ask that You give me the courage and endurance to keep on going through the testing situation in the comforting knowledge that I am not alone. You've promised me that You will never leave me nor forsake me in my time of trouble. In Jesus' name. Amen.

DAY 25 NOTES

BEAUTY FOR ASHES.

Ruth 3:11
'And now, my daughter, do not fear. I will do for you all that you request, for all the people of my town know that you are a virtuous woman.'

The definition of 'virtuous' is having or showing high moral standards. This is a very tall order to live up to but I can imagine that most people of God would like to define themselves as this type of person.

Being a virtuous person of God will often mean going against the status quo and what the world at large would view as popular. It may mean taking a stand by not partaking in activities that would compromise your moral standards. Making the decision not to compromise your moral standards may mean that the journey of life will often be lonely. People you thought were your closest friends may all of a sudden find reasons not to be available to see you. Usually, this is because you're not considered to be a 'fun' person anymore.

If you've ever had to decide to forsake all, be it family, friends, a job, a business deal, a proposition, or money so as to not compromise your moral standards then you'll know exactly what I'm talking about. It takes a lot of courage and conviction to make such a drastic stand and you will probably feel at a loss in the initial stages. However, over time you will have peace and a witness in your spirit that will act as the only confirmation that you'll need. Take heart, I've been sent to tell you that you have not made a mistake. Stick to what you believe is right and the Lord will openly reward you in ways you will never comprehend.

In the passage of scripture above, Ruth's reputation as a virtuous person preceded her. Boaz had heard all about her character and moral standing and as a result of her impeccable reputation, she was blessed with an honourable and loving husband. So, please make a decision not to compromise on any of your morals, beliefs, or standards because not only are people around you watching with eager eyes but, most importantly, the Lord is watching you with His eyes of love, compassion and understanding.

Prayer

Lord, I honour You today. I give You the praise, glory and all the adoration. You are worthy of all my praise because of all that You've chosen to bless me with. In particular, I thank You for the gift of virtue and for enabling me to be a person who can walk down this difficult, painful but worthwhile road. Walking down this road of virtue is not an easy one but with Your help, Lord, I know that I'll succeed because I recognise that everything is in Your hands. Father, I know that I'll have to rely on Your strength completely and not mine. Let Your will be done, Father God. In Jesus' name. Amen and amen.

DAY 26 NOTES

WISDOM IS THE PRINCIPAL THING.

James 1:5
'If any of you lacks wisdom, let him ask of God, who gives to all liberally and without reproach, and it will be given to him.'

Wisdom truly is the principal thing and can be defined in many ways. For instance, understanding, knowledge, perception, intelligence, and insightfulness. When all fails and you don't know what to do or which way to turn, step back and ask the Lord for wisdom. He will give it to you liberally. All you have to do is receive it and believe that you have been blessed with this amazing gift.

In the Bible, the Lord asked Solomon what he desired as a gift from Him. Solomon didn't ask for gold, silver, or money but for wisdom. God gave it to him and as a result, no one wiser than Solomon has walked the face of the earth since. In all honesty, who could have solved the dilemma of the child who was brought to Solomon by the two women who both claimed that the child was theirs?[1] This is a perfect example that demonstrates Solomon's gift of wisdom.

---

[1] *1 Kings 3: 16-21; 24-28*
Now two women who were harlots came to the king, and stood before him. One woman said, "O my lord, this woman and I dwell in the same house; and I gave birth while she was in the house. Then it happened, the third day after I had given birth, that this woman also gave birth. And we were together; no one was with us in the house, except the two of us in the house. And this woman's son died in the night, because she lay on him. So she arose in the middle of the night and took my son from my side, while your maidservant slept, and laid him in her bosom, and laid her dead child in my bosom. And when I rose in the morning to nurse my son, there he was, dead. But when I had examined him in the morning, indeed, he was not my son whom I had borne."

On the flip side, an example of two people in the Bible not using wisdom was Ananias and Sapphira. They both died immediately because, rather than tell the truth about how much they had been given for the sale of their land, they chose to lie to Peter, and ultimately, the Holy Spirit.

Prayer

Lord, You're bigger than my needs and wants. You've said in Your Word that wisdom is the principal thing. You said that if I lack wisdom then I should ask You for it and You will give it to me liberally and without reproach. Father, I choose to ask You to bless me with the gift of wisdom liberally and without reproach. Help me, Lord, to recognise that this gift is to be used without fear or reservation as everything that You give to me is perfect and therefore You have not given me this gift to feel reproach or shame. In Jesus' name. Amen.

Then the king said, "Bring me a sword." So they brought a sword before the king. And the king said, "Divide the living child in two, and give half to one, and half to the other."
Then the woman whose son was living spoke to the king, for she yearned with compassion for her son; and she said, "O my lord, give her the living child, and by no means kill him!"
But the other said, "Let him be neither mine nor yours, but divide him."
So the king answered and said, "Give the first woman the living child, and by no means kill him; she is his mother."
And all Israel heard of the judgment which the king had rendered; and they feared the king, for they saw that the wisdom of God was in him to administer justice.

DAY 27 NOTES

YOU ARE WORTH MORE THAN RUBIES.

Proverbs 3:15
'She is more precious than rubies, and all the things you may desire cannot compare with her.'

This scripture is so profound and I take these words as if the Lord is speaking to me personally. I would encourage you to do the same. The scripture tells us that the Lord values us beyond even our recognition. We cannot begin to fathom the depths of the Lord's love for us all. You are precious in His sight and you are more precious than rubies.

Rubies are considered to be the stone of love, energy, passion and power. The ruby, therefore, is the perfect symbol for powerful feelings and indeed in the Bible, it is considered the most precious of all gemstones. This further emphasises the Lord's undying feelings for us as He is saying that we are more valuable than the most precious gemstone on earth.

If you are a parent, take a few moments to reflect on how much you love your child or children. Now multiply that feeling by an infinite number and you would still not come anywhere close to how much you mean to the Lord.

I think that this scripture is so important because it serves to remind us in times when we're overcome with feelings of despair, that the Lord holds us forever dear to His heart and that we're not alone.

Prayer

Lord, I cannot begin to understand the depths of how You feel about me. But Heavenly Father, I thank You for seeing fit to value me far above the ruby which is the most precious gemstone on the face of the earth. This gives me a feeling of excitement and contentment as I am secure in the knowledge that you are right beside me loving and valuing me regardless of my thoughts, actions and shortcomings. In Jesus' name. Amen.

DAY 28 NOTES

SELF-CARE IS OKAY.

Luke 4:42
'Now when it was day, He departed and went into a deserted place…'

Self-care is a very interesting subject that is often overlooked in the busy times that we live in. We are often so busy looking after everyone else that we forget that we need to take time out to look after our own wellbeing.

In the scripture above, it is evident that even Jesus saw it fit to take time out of His very busy life to look after His own mental, physical and spiritual health. So, if it was good enough for Jesus to do then it's certainly good enough for us, His children.

Let's not get carried away with the ins and outs of what self-care involves. Just allow yourself to enjoy the moment. Self-care can be something as simple as painting your nails, escaping to the bathroom for a long-deserved soak, having a cup of tea while reading your favourite book, or going for a long walk with the dog. At the other end of the spectrum, there is taking a two-week holiday with friends or alone or even booking yourself a course of lessons in a subject that you've always wanted to learn more about. How about booking yourself some flying lessons or having a colon cleanse treatment? The list can go on and on but the point I'm making is that self-care needs to be an activity that you and only you enjoy. Even if it means going solo.

Self-care is about you re-energising yourself and boosting your mental, physical and spiritual health to be able to continue with life's journey in a more refreshed and calm manner. Your whole family will appreciate the new you and you most certainly will as well. I challenge you to initiate some form of regular self-care activity and when you begin to experience the benefits, I dare say that you will have no regrets that you made that life-changing decision.

Prayer

Heavenly Father, how amazing You are. You love me so much that you even show an interest in the smallest details of my life. Who would have thought that the details of how to take care of my mental and physical health would matter to You? You know me best so I ask, Father God, that You open my eyes to see what self-care activities You would have me take part in. In Jesus' name. Amen.

DAY 29 NOTES

YES, YOU CAN MAKE A STAND.

Numbers 27: 1, 3-5
'Then came the daughters of Zelophehad.... and he had no sons. Why should the name of our father be removed from among his family because he had no son? Give us a possession among our father's brothers." So Moses brought their case before the LORD.'

The daughters of Zelophehad must have been a formidable group of women. Can you imagine the courage it must have taken for them to make such a stand in the midst of all the men in their community? Women in biblical times were not allowed to inherit from their father's estate and because Zelophehad had no sons, their father's land was going to be divided amongst his brothers. This did not sit well with the five sisters and they decided to petition Moses to bring their case before the Lord.

This situation had never occurred before in Israel. However, by using wisdom and their ability to approach Moses with a humble spirit they managed to influence him to bring their petition to the Lord. The law was changed in their favour and for other women, in the future, who might find themselves in a similar position.

The reason why I wanted to use this example is to encourage you to realise that all things are possible through Jesus Christ, who strengthens you.[1] You walk in authority and power. You just have to receive it and believe it. Follow the example of the daughters of

---

[1] *Philippians 4:13*
I can do all things through Christ who strengthens me.

Zelophehad and pray for humility and wisdom. Then make your request known to the appropriate person, people, or organisation. You might very well surprise yourself in what you can achieve once the Lord is on your side.

Prayer

I come before You, Lord, to make my request known. I honour You today. I claim the same spirit of humility, wisdom, boldness, and courage that You blessed the daughters of Zelophehad with for myself, in Jesus' name. You know the situation, Father God, that I have on my heart where a miraculous change is needed. So, I'm thanking You in advance for the victory and, by faith, I'm decreeing and declaring that it has already been done. I believe it and receive it in the name of Jesus. Amen.

DAY 30 NOTES

_____

_____

_____

_____

_____

_____

_____

_____

_____

_____

_____

_____

_____

_____

_____

_____

_____

_____

_____

_____

_____

_____

HALLELUJAH, THE BEST NEWS OF ALL – IT'S OKAY TO FAIL AND TRY AGAIN. THE LORD IS A GOD OF SECOND CHANCES.

Exodus 2:14
'Then he said, "Who made you a prince and a judge over us? Do you intend to kill me as you killed the Egyptian?" So, Moses feared and said, "Surely this thing is known!"'

As the above title says, 'The Lord is a God of second chances.' Does that resonate with you? It certainly was true in the case of Moses, who besides Jesus, went on to be one of the greatest leaders in the whole Bible. You might ask yourself why the Lord would even consider using someone like Moses, who was a murderer. The same question would apply if you looked at other characters in the Bible such as David the adulterer, Elijah the coward, and Gideon the fearful one. But let's get personal – what about you?

The answer is very simply that the Lord has a plan and a purpose for your life.[1] You were not sent to this earth by accident. No matter where and how you were born, the Lord knew the circumstances beforehand because He was the one that allowed it. Remember that nothing surprises the Lord. He is an all-powerful and all-knowing God. Therefore, do not feel useless or unworthy for the Lord will use you when and how He sees fit. He knows the end from the beginning. You may be feeling worthless or as if the Lord could never use you in any capacity because of where you are at this time in your life or because of the things you've done in your past.

---

[1] *Jeremiah 29:11*
For I know the thoughts that I think toward you, says the LORD, thoughts of peace and not of evil, to give you a future and a hope.

I'm here to tell you that the Lord does things in His way so rest assured that you were born for such a time as this. Please do not be discouraged; just prayerfully go with the flow and allow the Lord to direct your path straight into your destiny.

Prayer

You are the all-knowing God Who knows all things and sees all things. I thank You today and I praise You for what You're about to do in my life. You know the end from the beginning and I just want to please You, Father God, in whatever way You lead and direct me. Help me, Lord, to recognise Your divine instruction for You say in Your Word, 'My sheep (children) hear my voice, and I know them, and they follow me.'[2] So, Father, give me the gift of being able to discern Your voice from all the other voices that are trying to take control of my mind. Once I have received Your divine instructions, I commit to following them with the knowledge that I cannot fail because You are with me every step of the way. In Jesus' name. Amen.

[2] *John 10:27*
My sheep hear My voice, and I know them, and they follow Me.

DAY 31 NOTES

FINAL THOUGHTS

Congratulations and well done now that you have journeyed with me through the past 31 days. You should be feeling delighted and very pleased with yourself as you've completed a key achievement in your journey to discover and fulfil your God-given purpose. You should be a lot more confident with who you are in Christ and have a clearer picture of why you were born. I would encourage you to start to take small daily steps in your new-found confidence and, in time, those small daily steps will start to produce the fruits that will manifest into your purpose.

I want you to remember that you are who God said you are, no matter the obstacles or the circumstances that you might currently find yourself in. No matter what people have to say to you, dust yourself down, brace yourself, pray, seek the Lord's guidance, and He will make a way even in the midst of adversity, because He has the final say.

In my own life, I've seen this time and time again where the Lord has made a way when I couldn't see how my breakthrough could possibly happen. There was a time in my life when I was completely broken, having gone through a very traumatic experience, and at my time of absolute need, the Lord led me to a church family who showed me unconditional love, which I had never experienced in all my years as a believer in Christ. This was at a time in my life when I had lost all faith in ever meeting genuine Christian brethren whose only agenda was to love and assist me along my journey to 'Regain Freedom'.

This example may not sound particularly extraordinary to you but I'm here to testify that the Lord most definitely sent these amazing people into my life when I was at my lowest spiritually, mentally and physically.

The Lord loves a challenge so put Him to the test and see if He won't guide and protect you through your time of healing, your time of deliverance, or whatever it is you need at this time. As you go through this period of your life, I urge you to always remember that the Lord said He will never leave you nor forsake you. (Deuteronomy 31:6)

I encourage you to keep this scripture at the forefront of your mind. As you do, at the end of your journey to 'Regain Freedom' you will have the victory and a testimony to share with others to inspire them along their own journey as they too 'Regain Freedom'. In Jesus' name. Amen and amen.

WOULD YOU LIKE TO BE A CHRISTIAN?

Would you like to invite Jesus Christ to be the Lord of your life and be that friend who will never leave you or forsake you? If this is the case, then it would be my pleasure to lead you in this simple prayer.

The Lord God says the following in the Holy Bible:

'Behold I stand at the door and knock. If anyone hears My voice and opens the door, I will come to him...' Revelations 3:20.

Now, repeat this short prayer aloud with a sincere heart...
Lord God, thank you for sending your son Jesus Christ to die on the cross for me. I believe that He rose from the dead and lives forevermore. I openly confess that Jesus Christ is the Son of God. Lord God I ask you to forgive me for all the sins that I have committed knowingly and unknowing. I ask you to come into my heart today and I also ask that you wash me in the Blood of Jesus to cleanse me from all unrighteousness. From this day forward I promise to serve you with a sincere and faithful heart.
In Jesus name. Amen.

If you have said this prayer, please get in touch using the email address below.

Jacqueline
regainfreedom22@gmail.com

ABOUT THE AUTHOR

Jacqueline Bent is an ordained minister of the Gospel and an itinerate speaker. For many years she pioneered and ran successful events called 'Set Down the Garment of Heaviness and Step into Purpose', which resulted in many, many attendees finding, fulfilling and to this day maintaining their purpose in life. Today she is a Life Purpose Coach and teaches at conferences, seminars and workshops that specialise in finding and fulfilling your purpose in life. Jacqueline has been gifted with the ability to draw out the best characteristics of those who choose to follow her practical and often very simple strategies, to find and fulfil their purpose. She is the proud mother of a son, Lorimar Joshua Charles and lives in London, UK.

Jacqueline can be contacted at regainfreedom22@gmail.com

Printed in Great Britain
by Amazon